A Workbook To Help Improve Your Penmanship & Handwriting Skills.

Perfect for Adults & Teens

This cute handwriting workbook belongs to:

Handwriting font sheet

By Nicole Elise

This is what my handwriting looked like on: /   /

This is what my handwriting looked like on: /   /

This is what my handwriting looked like on: /   /

Introduction

Handwriting is meant to be unique. I always felt like handwriting workbooks started with the largest print fonts (that are usually standard fonts you can download from google, or that you see on Microsoft Word), where you would only get around 3-7 lines per page to truly work with. I decided that it was time to invent a workbook that had font just a little bigger than the font you would usually write, but not so big that it felt unusual to practice with. The good thing for you is that this means per-page, there is more practice letters than most other handwriting workbooks. Win-win!

I have also added guides that breakdown the direction of each lowercase letter. If you have a different way of doing it, that is completely ok. Do what feels comfortable for you. This is just a starting point for those who would like a little more guidance.

Want free digital access to a PDF version of the blank practice sheet? (Yes. you do!)

Visit my Instagram @nicoleeliseprintables and click on the link in the description to be redirected to where you can download the free 'Cute & Neat' sheets for unlimited practice at home.

WHAT'S INSIDE

SECTION 1
Lowercase letters

Start here and learn the individual letters first

SECTION 2
Uppercase letters

Then progress to learning them together

SECTION 3
Combined Letter Practice

SECTION 4
Numbers

Progress to practicing writing full sentences. for your transition to free-hand writing

SECTION 5
Extra Word Practice

SECTION 6
Handwriting Tips & Prompts

View these for tips on pens. paper. posture. writing speed & more

SECTION 7
Blank Practice Sheets

Lowercase Letter Practice

Handwriting font sheet

By Nicole Elise

a a a a a a a a a a a a a a a a a a a a a a a a a a
a a a a a a a a a a a a a a a a a a a a a a a a a a
a a a a a a a a a a a a a a a a a a a a a a a a a a
a a a a a a a a a a a a a a a a a a a a a a a a a a
a a a a a a a a a a a a a a a a a a a a a a a a a a
a a a a a a a a a a a a a a a a a a a a a a a a a a
a a a a a a a a a a a a a a a a a a a a a a a a a a
a a a a a a a a a a a a a a a a a a a a a a a a a a
a a a a a a a a a a a a a a a a a a a a a a a a a a
a a a a a a a a a a a a a a a a a a a a a a a a a a
a a a a a a a a a a a a a a a a a a a a a a a a a a
a a a a a a a a a a a a a a a a a a a a a a a a a a
a a a a a a a a a a a a a a a a a a a a a a a a a a
a a a a a a a a a a a a a a a a a a a a a a a a a a
a a a a a a a a a a a a a a a a a a a a a a a a a a
a a a a a a a a a a a a a a a a a a a a a a a a a a
a a a a a a a a a a a a a a a a a a a a a a a a a a

Handwriting font sheet

By Nicole Elise

b b b b b b b b b b b b b b b b b b b b b b b b

b b b b b b b b b b b b b b b b b b b b b b b b

b b b b b b b b b b b b b b b b b b b b b b b b

b b b b b b b b b b b b b b b b b b b b b b b b

b b b b b b b b b b b b b b b b b b b b b b b b

b b b b b b b b b b b b b b b b b b b b b b b b

b b b b b b b b b b b b b b b b b b b b b b b b

b b b b b b b b b b b b b b b b b b b b b b b b

b b b b b b b b b b b b b b b b b b b b b b b b

b b b b b b b b b b b b b b b b b b b b b b b b

b b b b b b b b b b b b b b b b b b b b b b b b

b b b b b b b b b b b b b b b b b b b b b b b b

b b b b b b b b b b b b b b b b b b b b b b b b

b b b b b b b b b b b b b b b b b b b b b b b b

b b b b b b b b b b b b b b b b b b b b b b b b

b b b b b b b b b b b b b b b b b b b b b b b b

Handwriting font sheet

By Nicole Elise

C C C C C C C C C C C C C C C C C C C C C C C C

C C C C C C C C C C C C C C C C C C C C C C C C

C C C C C C C C C C C C C C C C C C C C C C C C

C C C C C C C C C C C C C C C C C C C C C C C C

C C C C C C C C C C C C C C C C C C C C C C C C

C C C C C C C C C C C C C C C C C C C C C C C C

C C C C C C C C C C C C C C C C C C C C C C C C

C C C C C C C C C C C C C C C C C C C C C C C C

C C C C C C C C C C C C C C C C C C C C C C C C

C C C C C C C C C C C C C C C C C C C C C C C C

C C C C C C C C C C C C C C C C C C C C C C C C

C C C C C C C C C C C C C C C C C C C C C C C C

C C C C C C C C C C C C C C C C C C C C C C C C

C C C C C C C C C C C C C C C C C C C C C C C C

C C C C C C C C C C C C C C C C C C C C C C C C

C C C C C C C C C C C C C C C C C C C C C C C C

Handwriting font sheet

By Nicole Elise

d d d d d d d d d d d d d d d d d d d d d d d d d d d

d d d d d d d d d d d d d d d d d d d d d d d d d d d

d d d d d d d d d d d d d d d d d d d d d d d d d d d

d d d d d d d d d d d d d d d d d d d d d d d d d d d

d d d d d d d d d d d d d d d d d d d d d d d d d d d

d d d d d d d d d d d d d d d d d d d d d d d d d d d

d d d d d d d d d d d d d d d d d d d d d d d d d d d

d d d d d d d d d d d d d d d d d d d d d d d d d d d

d d d d d d d d d d d d d d d d d d d d d d d d d d d

d d d d d d d d d d d d d d d d d d d d d d d d d d d

d d d d d d d d d d d d d d d d d d d d d d d d d d d

d d d d d d d d d d d d d d d d d d d d d d d d d d d

d d d d d d d d d d d d d d d d d d d d d d d d d d d

d d d d d d d d d d d d d d d d d d d d d d d d d d d

d d d d d d d d d d d d d d d d d d d d d d d d d d d

Handwriting font sheet

By Nicole Elise

e e e e e e e e e e e e e e e e e e e e e e e e e e

e e e e e e e e e e e e e e e e e e e e e e e e e e

e e e e e e e e e e e e e e e e e e e e e e e e e e

e e e e e e e e e e e e e e e e e e e e e e e e e e

e e e e e e e e e e e e e e e e e e e e e e e e e e

e e e e e e e e e e e e e e e e e e e e e e e e e e

e e e e e e e e e e e e e e e e e e e e e e e e e e

e e e e e e e e e e e e e e e e e e e e e e e e e e

e e e e e e e e e e e e e e e e e e e e e e e e e e

e e e e e e e e e e e e e e e e e e e e e e e e e e

e e e e e e e e e e e e e e e e e e e e e e e e e e

e e e e e e e e e e e e e e e e e e e e e e e e e e

e e e e e e e e e e e e e e e e e e e e e e e e e e

e e e e e e e e e e e e e e e e e e e e e e e e e e

e e e e e e e e e e e e e e e e e e e e e e e e e e

e e e e e e e e e e e e e e e e e e e e e e e e e e

Handwriting font sheet

By Nicole Elise

Handwriting font sheet

By Nicole Elise

g g g g g g g g g g g g g g g g g g g g g g g g
g g g g g g g g g g g g g g g g g g g g g g g g
g g g g g g g g g g g g g g g g g g g g g g g g
g g g g g g g g g g g g g g g g g g g g g g g g
g g g g g g g g g g g g g g g g g g g g g g g g
g g g g g g g g g g g g g g g g g g g g g g g g
g g g g g g g g g g g g g g g g g g g g g g g g
g g g g g g g g g g g g g g g g g g g g g g g g
g g g g g g g g g g g g g g g g g g g g g g g g
g g g g g g g g g g g g g g g g g g g g g g g g
g g g g g g g g g g g g g g g g g g g g g g g g
g g g g g g g g g g g g g g g g g g g g g g g g
g g g g g g g g g g g g g g g g g g g g g g g g
g g g g g g g g g g g g g g g g g g g g g g g g
g g g g g g g g g g g g g g g g g g g g g g g g
g g g g g g g g g g g g g g g g g g g g g g g g

Handwriting font sheet

By Nicole Elise

h h h h h h h h h h h h h h h h h h h h
h h h h h h h h h h h h h h h h h h h h
h h h h h h h h h h h h h h h h h h h h
h h h h h h h h h h h h h h h h h h h h
h h h h h h h h h h h h h h h h h h h h
h h h h h h h h h h h h h h h h h h h h
h h h h h h h h h h h h h h h h h h h h
h h h h h h h h h h h h h h h h h h h h
h h h h h h h h h h h h h h h h h h h h
h h h h h h h h h h h h h h h h h h h h
h h h h h h h h h h h h h h h h h h h h
h h h h h h h h h h h h h h h h h h h h
h h h h h h h h h h h h h h h h h h h h
h h h h h h h h h h h h h h h h h h h h
h h h h h h h h h h h h h h h h h h h h
h h h h h h h h h h h h h h h h h h h h

Handwriting font sheet

By Nicole Elise

i i i i i i i i i i i i i i i i i i i i i i i i i i i i i

i i i i i i i i i i i i i i i i i i i i i i i i i i i i i

i i i i i i i i i i i i i i i i i i i i i i i i i i i i i

i i i i i i i i i i i i i i i i i i i i i i i i i i i i i

i i i i i i i i i i i i i i i i i i i i i i i i i i i i i

i i i i i i i i i i i i i i i i i i i i i i i i i i i i i

i i i i i i i i i i i i i i i i i i i i i i i i i i i i i

i i i i i i i i i i i i i i i i i i i i i i i i i i i i i

i i i i i i i i i i i i i i i i i i i i i i i i i i i i i

i i i i i i i i i i i i i i i i i i i i i i i i i i i i i

i i i i i i i i i i i i i i i i i i i i i i i i i i i i i

i i i i i i i i i i i i i i i i i i i i i i i i i i i i i

i i i i i i i i i i i i i i i i i i i i i i i i i i i i i

i i i i i i i i i i i i i i i i i i i i i i i i i i i i i

i i i i i i i i i i i i i i i i i i i i i i i i i i i i i

i i i i i i i i i i i i i i i i i i i i i i i i i i i i i

Handwriting font sheet

By Nicole Elise

j j j j j j j j j j j j j j j j j j j j j j j j j j j j j j j j j j j j

j j j j j j j j j j j j j j j j j j j j j j j j j j j j j j j j j j j j

j j j j j j j j j j j j j j j j j j j j j j j j j j j j j j j j j j j j

j j j j j j j j j j j j j j j j j j j j j j j j j j j j j j j j j j j j

j j j j j j j j j j j j j j j j j j j j j j j j j j j j j j j j j j j j

j j j j j j j j j j j j j j j j j j j j j j j j j j j j j j j j j j j j

j j j j j j j j j j j j j j j j j j j j j j j j j j j j j j j j j j j j

j j j j j j j j j j j j j j j j j j j j j j j j j j j j j j j j j j j j

j j j j j j j j j j j j j j j j j j j j j j j j j j j j j j j j j j j j

j j j j j j j j j j j j j j j j j j j j j j j j j j j j j j j j j j j j

j j j j j j j j j j j j j j j j j j j j j j j j j j j j j j j j j j j j

j j j j j j j j j j j j j j j j j j j j j j j j j j j j j j j j j j j j

j j j j j j j j j j j j j j j j j j j j j j j j j j j j j j j j j j j j

j j j j j j j j j j j j j j j j j j j j j j j j j j j j j j j j j j j j

j j j j j j j j j j j j j j j j j j j j j j j j j j j j j j j j j j j j

j j j j j j j j j j j j j j j j j j j j j j j j j j j j j j j j j j j j

Handwriting font sheet

By Nicole Elise

k k k k k k k k k k k k k k k k k k k k
k k k k k k k k k k k k k k k k k k k k
k k k k k k k k k k k k k k k k k k k k
k k k k k k k k k k k k k k k k k k k k
k k k k k k k k k k k k k k k k k k k k
k k k k k k k k k k k k k k k k k k k k
k k k k k k k k k k k k k k k k k k k k
k k k k k k k k k k k k k k k k k k k k
k k k k k k k k k k k k k k k k k k k k
k k k k k k k k k k k k k k k k k k k k
k k k k k k k k k k k k k k k k k k k k
k k k k k k k k k k k k k k k k k k k k
k k k k k k k k k k k k k k k k k k k k
k k k k k k k k k k k k k k k k k k k k
k k k k k k k k k k k k k k k k k k k k
k k k k k k k k k k k k k k k k k k k k

Handwriting font sheet

By Nicole Elise

1 ↓||

| | | | | | | | | | | | | | | | | | | | | | | | | | | | | | | | | | | | | | | | | | | | | |

| | | | | | | | | | | | | | | | | | | | | | | | | | | | | | | | | | | | | | | | | | | |

| | | | | | | | | | | | | | | | | | | | | | | | | | | | | | | | | | | | | | | | | | | |

| | | | | | | | | | | | | | | | | | | | | | | | | | | | | | | | | | | | | | | | | | | |

| | | | | | | | | | | | | | | | | | | | | | | | | | | | | | | | | | | | | | | | | | | |

| | | | | | | | | | | | | | | | | | | | | | | | | | | | | | | | | | | | | | | | | | | |

| | | | | | | | | | | | | | | | | | | | | | | | | | | | | | | | | | | | | | | | | | | |

| | | | | | | | | | | | | | | | | | | | | | | | | | | | | | | | | | | | | | | | | | | |

| | | | | | | | | | | | | | | | | | | | | | | | | | | | | | | | | | | | | | | | | | | |

| | | | | | | | | | | | | | | | | | | | | | | | | | | | | | | | | | | | | | | | | | | |

| | | | | | | | | | | | | | | | | | | | | | | | | | | | | | | | | | | | | | | | | | | |

| | | | | | | | | | | | | | | | | | | | | | | | | | | | | | | | | | | | | | | | | | | |

| | | | | | | | | | | | | | | | | | | | | | | | | | | | | | | | | | | | | | | | | | | |

| | | | | | | | | | | | | | | | | | | | | | | | | | | | | | | | | | | | | | | | | | | |

| | | | | | | | | | | | | | | | | | | | | | | | | | | | | | | | | | | | | | | | | | | |

| | | | | | | | | | | | | | | | | | | | | | | | | | | | | | | | | | | | | | | | | | | |

Handwriting font sheet

By Nicole Elise

1 ↓m 2 3

m m m m m m m m m m m m m m m m m m m m m m m
m m m m m m m m m m m m m m m m m m m m m m m
m m m m m m m m m m m m m m m m m m m m m m m
m m m m m m m m m m m m m m m m m m m m m m m
m m m m m m m m m m m m m m m m m m m m m m m
m m m m m m m m m m m m m m m m m m m m m m m
m m m m m m m m m m m m m m m m m m m m m m m
m m m m m m m m m m m m m m m m m m m m m m m
m m m m m m m m m m m m m m m m m m m m m m m
m m m m m m m m m m m m m m m m m m m m m m m
m m m m m m m m m m m m m m m m m m m m m m m
m m m m m m m m m m m m m m m m m m m m m m m
m m m m m m m m m m m m m m m m m m m m m m m
m m m m m m m m m m m m m m m m m m m m m m m
m m m m m m m m m m m m m m m m m m m m m m m
m m m m m m m m m m m m m m m m m m m m m m m
m m m m m m m m m m m m m m m m m m m m m m m

$_1\downarrow n \downarrow^2$

n n n n n n n n n n n n n n n n n n n
n n n n n n n n n n n n n n n n n n n
n n n n n n n n n n n n n n n n n n n
n n n n n n n n n n n n n n n n n n n
n n n n n n n n n n n n n n n n n n n
n n n n n n n n n n n n n n n n n n n
n n n n n n n n n n n n n n n n n n n
n n n n n n n n n n n n n n n n n n n
n n n n n n n n n n n n n n n n n n n
n n n n n n n n n n n n n n n n n n n
n n n n n n n n n n n n n n n n n n n
n n n n n n n n n n n n n n n n n n n
n n n n n n n n n n n n n n n n n n n
n n n n n n n n n n n n n n n n n n n
n n n n n n n n n n n n n n n n n n n
n n n n n n n n n n n n n n n n n n n

Handwriting font sheet

By Nicole Elise

0 0 0 0 0 0 0 0 0 0 0 0 0 0 0 0 0 0 0 0 0 0 0

0 0 0 0 0 0 0 0 0 0 0 0 0 0 0 0 0 0 0 0 0 0 0

0 0 0 0 0 0 0 0 0 0 0 0 0 0 0 0 0 0 0 0 0 0 0

0 0 0 0 0 0 0 0 0 0 0 0 0 0 0 0 0 0 0 0 0 0 0

0 0 0 0 0 0 0 0 0 0 0 0 0 0 0 0 0 0 0 0 0 0 0

0 0 0 0 0 0 0 0 0 0 0 0 0 0 0 0 0 0 0 0 0 0 0

0 0 0 0 0 0 0 0 0 0 0 0 0 0 0 0 0 0 0 0 0 0 0

0 0 0 0 0 0 0 0 0 0 0 0 0 0 0 0 0 0 0 0 0 0 0

0 0 0 0 0 0 0 0 0 0 0 0 0 0 0 0 0 0 0 0 0 0 0

0 0 0 0 0 0 0 0 0 0 0 0 0 0 0 0 0 0 0 0 0 0 0

0 0 0 0 0 0 0 0 0 0 0 0 0 0 0 0 0 0 0 0 0 0 0

0 0 0 0 0 0 0 0 0 0 0 0 0 0 0 0 0 0 0 0 0 0 0

0 0 0 0 0 0 0 0 0 0 0 0 0 0 0 0 0 0 0 0 0 0 0

0 0 0 0 0 0 0 0 0 0 0 0 0 0 0 0 0 0 0 0 0 0 0

0 0 0 0 0 0 0 0 0 0 0 0 0 0 0 0 0 0 0 0 0 0 0

0 0 0 0 0 0 0 0 0 0 0 0 0 0 0 0 0 0 0 0 0 0 0

Handwriting font sheet

By Nicole Elise

p p p p p p p p p p p p p p p p p p p p p p p p

p p p p p p p p p p p p p p p p p p p p p p p p

p p p p p p p p p p p p p p p p p p p p p p p p

p p p p p p p p p p p p p p p p p p p p p p p p

p p p p p p p p p p p p p p p p p p p p p p p p

p p p p p p p p p p p p p p p p p p p p p p p p

p p p p p p p p p p p p p p p p p p p p p p p p

p p p p p p p p p p p p p p p p p p p p p p p p

p p p p p p p p p p p p p p p p p p p p p p p p

p p p p p p p p p p p p p p p p p p p p p p p p

p p p p p p p p p p p p p p p p p p p p p p p p

p p p p p p p p p p p p p p p p p p p p p p p p

p p p p p p p p p p p p p p p p p p p p p p p p

p p p p p p p p p p p p p p p p p p p p p p p p

p p p p p p p p p p p p p p p p p p p p p p p p

p p p p p p p p p p p p p p p p p p p p p p p p

Handwriting font sheet

By Nicole Elise

q q q q q q q q q q q q q q q q q q q q

q q q q q q q q q q q q q q q q q q q q

q q q q q q q q q q q q q q q q q q q q

q q q q q q q q q q q q q q q q q q q q

q q q q q q q q q q q q q q q q q q q q

q q q q q q q q q q q q q q q q q q q q

q q q q q q q q q q q q q q q q q q q q

q q q q q q q q q q q q q q q q q q q q

q q q q q q q q q q q q q q q q q q q q

q q q q q q q q q q q q q q q q q q q q

q q q q q q q q q q q q q q q q q q q q

q q q q q q q q q q q q q q q q q q q q

q q q q q q q q q q q q q q q q q q q q

q q q q q q q q q q q q q q q q q q q q

q q q q q q q q q q q q q q q q q q q q

q q q q q q q q q q q q q q q q q q q q

q q q q q q q q q q q q q q q q q q q q

q q q q q q q q q q q q q q q q q q q q

Handwriting font sheet

By Nicole Elise

r r r r r r r r r r r r r r r r r r r r r r r r r r r r r r

r r r r r r r r r r r r r r r r r r r r r r r r r r r r r r

r r r r r r r r r r r r r r r r r r r r r r r r r r r r r r

r r r r r r r r r r r r r r r r r r r r r r r r r r r r r r

r r r r r r r r r r r r r r r r r r r r r r r r r r r r r r

r r r r r r r r r r r r r r r r r r r r r r r r r r r r r r

r r r r r r r r r r r r r r r r r r r r r r r r r r r r r r

r r r r r r r r r r r r r r r r r r r r r r r r r r r r r r

r r r r r r r r r r r r r r r r r r r r r r r r r r r r r r

r r r r r r r r r r r r r r r r r r r r r r r r r r r r r r

r r r r r r r r r r r r r r r r r r r r r r r r r r r r r r

r r r r r r r r r r r r r r r r r r r r r r r r r r r r r r

r r r r r r r r r r r r r r r r r r r r r r r r r r r r r r

r r r r r r r r r r r r r r r r r r r r r r r r r r r r r r

r r r r r r r r r r r r r r r r r r r r r r r r r r r r r r

r r r r r r r r r r r r r r r r r r r r r r r r r r r r r r

Handwriting font sheet

By Nicole Elise

S S S S S S S S S S S S S S S S S S S S S

S S S S S S S S S S S S S S S S S S S S S

S S S S S S S S S S S S S S S S S S S S S

S S S S S S S S S S S S S S S S S S S S S

S S S S S S S S S S S S S S S S S S S S S

S S S S S S S S S S S S S S S S S S S S S

S S S S S S S S S S S S S S S S S S S S S

S S S S S S S S S S S S S S S S S S S S S

S S S S S S S S S S S S S S S S S S S S S

S S S S S S S S S S S S S S S S S S S S S

S S S S S S S S S S S S S S S S S S S S S

S S S S S S S S S S S S S S S S S S S S S

S S S S S S S S S S S S S S S S S S S S S

S S S S S S S S S S S S S S S S S S S S S

S S S S S S S S S S S S S S S S S S S S S

S S S S S S S S S S S S S S S S S S S S S

Handwriting font sheet

By Nicole Elise

† †
† †
† †
† †
† †
† †
† †
† †
† †
† †
† †
† †
† †
† †
† †
† †

Handwriting font sheet

By Nicole Elise

u u u u u u u u u u u u u u u u u u u u u

u u u u u u u u u u u u u u u u u u u u u

u u u u u u u u u u u u u u u u u u u u u

u u u u u u u u u u u u u u u u u u u u u

u u u u u u u u u u u u u u u u u u u u u

u u u u u u u u u u u u u u u u u u u u u

u u u u u u u u u u u u u u u u u u u u u

u u u u u u u u u u u u u u u u u u u u u

u u u u u u u u u u u u u u u u u u u u u

u u u u u u u u u u u u u u u u u u u u u

u u u u u u u u u u u u u u u u u u u u u

u u u u u u u u u u u u u u u u u u u u u

u u u u u u u u u u u u u u u u u u u u u

u u u u u u u u u u u u u u u u u u u u u

u u u u u u u u u u u u u u u u u u u u u

u u u u u u u u u u u u u u u u u u u u u

1 ↓ V ↑ 2

V V V V V V V V V V V V V V V V V V V V V V V V V V
V V V V V V V V V V V V V V V V V V V V V V V V V V
V V V V V V V V V V V V V V V V V V V V V V V V V V
V V V V V V V V V V V V V V V V V V V V V V V V V V
V V V V V V V V V V V V V V V V V V V V V V V V V V
V V V V V V V V V V V V V V V V V V V V V V V V V V
V V V V V V V V V V V V V V V V V V V V V V V V V V
V V V V V V V V V V V V V V V V V V V V V V V V V V
V V V V V V V V V V V V V V V V V V V V V V V V V V
V V V V V V V V V V V V V V V V V V V V V V V V V V
V V V V V V V V V V V V V V V V V V V V V V V V V V
V V V V V V V V V V V V V V V V V V V V V V V V V V
V V V V V V V V V V V V V V V V V V V V V V V V V V
V V V V V V V V V V V V V V V V V V V V V V V V V V
V V V V V V V V V V V V V V V V V V V V V V V V V V
V V V V V V V V V V V V V V V V V V V V V V V V V V
V V V V V V V V V V V V V V V V V V V V V V V V V V

Handwriting font sheet

W W W W W W W W W W W W W W W W W W W W W W W W W
W W W W W W W W W W W W W W W W W W W W W W W W W
W W W W W W W W W W W W W W W W W W W W W W W W W
W W W W W W W W W W W W W W W W W W W W W W W W W
W W W W W W W W W W W W W W W W W W W W W W W W W
W W W W W W W W W W W W W W W W W W W W W W W W W
W W W W W W W W W W W W W W W W W W W W W W W W W
W W W W W W W W W W W W W W W W W W W W W W W W W
W W W W W W W W W W W W W W W W W W W W W W W W W
W W W W W W W W W W W W W W W W W W W W W W W W W
W W W W W W W W W W W W W W W W W W W W W W W W W
W W W W W W W W W W W W W W W W W W W W W W W W W
W W W W W W W W W W W W W W W W W W W W W W W W W
W W W W W W W W W W W W W W W W W W W W W W W W W
W W W W W W W W W W W W W W W W W W W W W W W W W
W W W W W W W W W W W W W W W W W W W W W W W W W

Handwriting font sheet

By Nicole Elise

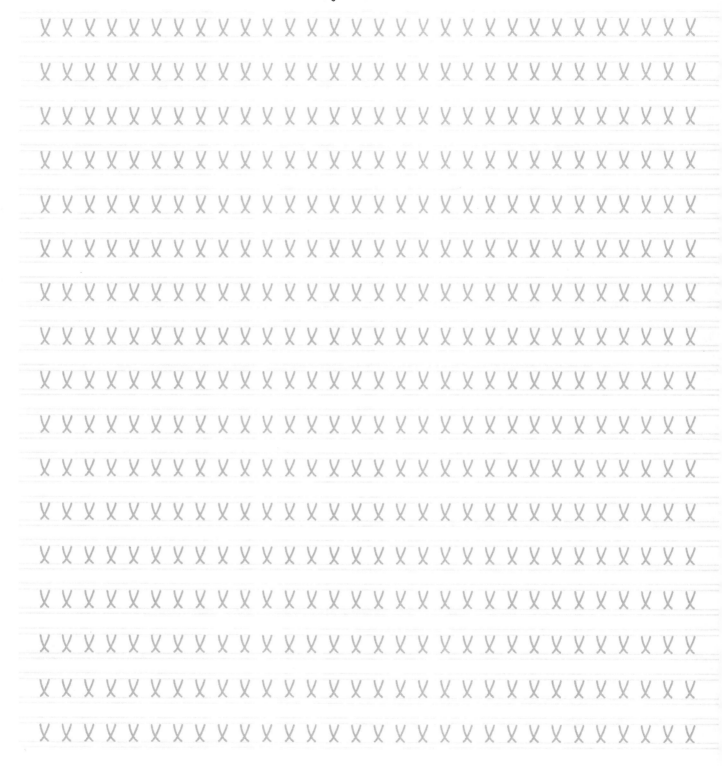

Handwriting font sheet

By Nicole Elise

y y y y y y y y y y y y y y y y y y y y y y y y
y y y y y y y y y y y y y y y y y y y y y y y y
y y y y y y y y y y y y y y y y y y y y y y y y
y y y y y y y y y y y y y y y y y y y y y y y y
y y y y y y y y y y y y y y y y y y y y y y y y
y y y y y y y y y y y y y y y y y y y y y y y y
y y y y y y y y y y y y y y y y y y y y y y y y
y y y y y y y y y y y y y y y y y y y y y y y y
y y y y y y y y y y y y y y y y y y y y y y y y
y y y y y y y y y y y y y y y y y y y y y y y y
y y y y y y y y y y y y y y y y y y y y y y y y
y y y y y y y y y y y y y y y y y y y y y y y y
y y y y y y y y y y y y y y y y y y y y y y y y
y y y y y y y y y y y y y y y y y y y y y y y y
y y y y y y y y y y y y y y y y y y y y y y y y
y y y y y y y y y y y y y y y y y y y y y y y y

Handwriting font sheet

By Nicole Elise

3 3 3 3 3 3 3 3 3 3 3 3 3 3 3 3 3 3 3 3 3 3 3 3 3

3 3 3 3 3 3 3 3 3 3 3 3 3 3 3 3 3 3 3 3 3 3 3 3 3

3 3 3 3 3 3 3 3 3 3 3 3 3 3 3 3 3 3 3 3 3 3 3 3 3

3 3 3 3 3 3 3 3 3 3 3 3 3 3 3 3 3 3 3 3 3 3 3 3 3

3 3 3 3 3 3 3 3 3 3 3 3 3 3 3 3 3 3 3 3 3 3 3 3 3

3 3 3 3 3 3 3 3 3 3 3 3 3 3 3 3 3 3 3 3 3 3 3 3 3

3 3 3 3 3 3 3 3 3 3 3 3 3 3 3 3 3 3 3 3 3 3 3 3 3

3 3 3 3 3 3 3 3 3 3 3 3 3 3 3 3 3 3 3 3 3 3 3 3 3

3 3 3 3 3 3 3 3 3 3 3 3 3 3 3 3 3 3 3 3 3 3 3 3 3

3 3 3 3 3 3 3 3 3 3 3 3 3 3 3 3 3 3 3 3 3 3 3 3 3

3 3 3 3 3 3 3 3 3 3 3 3 3 3 3 3 3 3 3 3 3 3 3 3 3

3 3 3 3 3 3 3 3 3 3 3 3 3 3 3 3 3 3 3 3 3 3 3 3 3

3 3 3 3 3 3 3 3 3 3 3 3 3 3 3 3 3 3 3 3 3 3 3 3 3

3 3 3 3 3 3 3 3 3 3 3 3 3 3 3 3 3 3 3 3 3 3 3 3 3

3 3 3 3 3 3 3 3 3 3 3 3 3 3 3 3 3 3 3 3 3 3 3 3 3

3 3 3 3 3 3 3 3 3 3 3 3 3 3 3 3 3 3 3 3 3 3 3 3 3

Uppercase Letter Practice

Handwriting font sheet

A A A A A A A A A A A A A A A A A A A A A A A A

A A A A A A A A A A A A A A A A A A A A A A A A

A A A A A A A A A A A A A A A A A A A A A A A A

A A A A A A A A A A A A A A A A A A A A A A A A

A A A A A A A A A A A A A A A A A A A A A A A A

A A A A A A A A A A A A A A A A A A A A A A A A

A A A A A A A A A A A A A A A A A A A A A A A A

A A A A A A A A A A A A A A A A A A A A A A A A

A A A A A A A A A A A A A A A A A A A A A A A A

A A A A A A A A A A A A A A A A A A A A A A A A

A A A A A A A A A A A A A A A A A A A A A A A A

A A A A A A A A A A A A A A A A A A A A A A A A

A A A A A A A A A A A A A A A A A A A A A A A A

A A A A A A A A A A A A A A A A A A A A A A A A

A A A A A A A A A A A A A A A A A A A A A A A A

A A A A A A A A A A A A A A A A A A A A A A A A

A A A A A A A A A A A A A A A A A A A A A A A A

Handwriting font sheet

Nicole Elise Design

Handwriting font sheet

C C C C C C C C C C C C C C C C C C C C C C C C C
C C C C C C C C C C C C C C C C C C C C C C C C C
C C C C C C C C C C C C C C C C C C C C C C C C C
C C C C C C C C C C C C C C C C C C C C C C C C C
C C C C C C C C C C C C C C C C C C C C C C C C C
C C C C C C C C C C C C C C C C C C C C C C C C C
C C C C C C C C C C C C C C C C C C C C C C C C C
C C C C C C C C C C C C C C C C C C C C C C C C C
C C C C C C C C C C C C C C C C C C C C C C C C C
C C C C C C C C C C C C C C C C C C C C C C C C C
C C C C C C C C C C C C C C C C C C C C C C C C C
C C C C C C C C C C C C C C C C C C C C C C C C C
C C C C C C C C C C C C C C C C C C C C C C C C C
C C C C C C C C C C C C C C C C C C C C C C C C C
C C C C C C C C C C C C C C C C C C C C C C C C C
C C C C C C C C C C C C C C C C C C C C C C C C C
C C C C C C C C C C C C C C C C C C C C C C C C C

Handwriting font sheet

Nicole Elise Design

Handwriting font sheet

Nicole Elise Design

E E E E E E E E E E E E E E E E E E E E E E E E E
E E E E E E E E E E E E E E E E E E E E E E E E E
E E E E E E E E E E E E E E E E E E E E E E E E E
E E E E E E E E E E E E E E E E E E E E E E E E E
E E E E E E E E E E E E E E E E E E E E E E E E E
E E E E E E E E E E E E E E E E E E E E E E E E E
E E E E E E E E E E E E E E E E E E E E E E E E E
E E E E E E E E E E E E E E E E E E E E E E E E E
E E E E E E E E E E E E E E E E E E E E E E E E E
E E E E E E E E E E E E E E E E E E E E E E E E E
E E E E E E E E E E E E E E E E E E E E E E E E E
E E E E E E E E E E E E E E E E E E E E E E E E E
E E E E E E E E E E E E E E E E E E E E E E E E E
E E E E E E E E E E E E E E E E E E E E E E E E E
E E E E E E E E E E E E E E E E E E E E E E E E E
E E E E E E E E E E E E E E E E E E E E E E E E E
E E E E E E E E E E E E E E E E E E E E E E E E E

Handwriting font sheet

—— Nicole Elise Design ——

F F F F F F F F F F F F F F F F F F F F
F F F F F F F F F F F F F F F F F F F F
F F F F F F F F F F F F F F F F F F F F
F F F F F F F F F F F F F F F F F F F F
F F F F F F F F F F F F F F F F F F F F
F F F F F F F F F F F F F F F F F F F F
F F F F F F F F F F F F F F F F F F F F
F F F F F F F F F F F F F F F F F F F F
F F F F F F F F F F F F F F F F F F F F
F F F F F F F F F F F F F F F F F F F F
F F F F F F F F F F F F F F F F F F F F
F F F F F F F F F F F F F F F F F F F F
F F F F F F F F F F F F F F F F F F F F
F F F F F F F F F F F F F F F F F F F F
F F F F F F F F F F F F F F F F F F F F
F F F F F F F F F F F F F F F F F F F F
F F F F F F F F F F F F F F F F F F F F

Handwriting font sheet

—— Nicole Elise Design ——

G G G G G G G G G G G G G G G G G G G G G G G G G G
G G G G G G G G G G G G G G G G G G G G G G G G G G
G G G G G G G G G G G G G G G G G G G G G G G G G G
G G G G G G G G G G G G G G G G G G G G G G G G G G
G G G G G G G G G G G G G G G G G G G G G G G G G G
G G G G G G G G G G G G G G G G G G G G G G G G G G
G G G G G G G G G G G G G G G G G G G G G G G G G G
G G G G G G G G G G G G G G G G G G G G G G G G G G
G G G G G G G G G G G G G G G G G G G G G G G G G G
G G G G G G G G G G G G G G G G G G G G G G G G G G
G G G G G G G G G G G G G G G G G G G G G G G G G G
G G G G G G G G G G G G G G G G G G G G G G G G G G
G G G G G G G G G G G G G G G G G G G G G G G G G G
G G G G G G G G G G G G G G G G G G G G G G G G G G
G G G G G G G G G G G G G G G G G G G G G G G G G G
G G G G G G G G G G G G G G G G G G G G G G G G G G

Handwriting font sheet

—— Nicole Elise Design ——

H H H H H H H H H H H H H H H H H H H H H H H H H

H H H H H H H H H H H H H H H H H H H H H H H H H

H H H H H H H H H H H H H H H H H H H H H H H H H

H H H H H H H H H H H H H H H H H H H H H H H H H

H H H H H H H H H H H H H H H H H H H H H H H H H

H H H H H H H H H H H H H H H H H H H H H H H H H

H H H H H H H H H H H H H H H H H H H H H H H H H

H H H H H H H H H H H H H H H H H H H H H H H H H

H H H H H H H H H H H H H H H H H H H H H H H H H

H H H H H H H H H H H H H H H H H H H H H H H H H

H H H H H H H H H H H H H H H H H H H H H H H H H

H H H H H H H H H H H H H H H H H H H H H H H H H

H H H H H H H H H H H H H H H H H H H H H H H H H

H H H H H H H H H H H H H H H H H H H H H H H H H

H H H H H H H H H H H H H H H H H H H H H H H H H

H H H H H H H H H H H H H H H H H H H H H H H H H

H H H H H H H H H H H H H H H H H H H H H H H H H

Handwriting font sheet

Nicole Elise Design

I I I I I I I I I I I I I I I I I I I I I I I I I I I I I
I I I I I I I I I I I I I I I I I I I I I I I I I I I I I
I I I I I I I I I I I I I I I I I I I I I I I I I I I I I
I I I I I I I I I I I I I I I I I I I I I I I I I I I I I
I I I I I I I I I I I I I I I I I I I I I I I I I I I I I
I I I I I I I I I I I I I I I I I I I I I I I I I I I I I
I I I I I I I I I I I I I I I I I I I I I I I I I I I I I
I I I I I I I I I I I I I I I I I I I I I I I I I I I I I
I I I I I I I I I I I I I I I I I I I I I I I I I I I I I
I I I I I I I I I I I I I I I I I I I I I I I I I I I I I
I I I I I I I I I I I I I I I I I I I I I I I I I I I I I
I I I I I I I I I I I I I I I I I I I I I I I I I I I I I
I I I I I I I I I I I I I I I I I I I I I I I I I I I I I
I I I I I I I I I I I I I I I I I I I I I I I I I I I I I
I I I I I I I I I I I I I I I I I I I I I I I I I I I I I
I I I I I I I I I I I I I I I I I I I I I I I I I I I I I

Handwriting font sheet

Nicole Elise Design

J J J J J J J J J J J J J J J J J J J J J J J J J J

J J J J J J J J J J J J J J J J J J J J J J J J J J

J J J J J J J J J J J J J J J J J J J J J J J J J J

J J J J J J J J J J J J J J J J J J J J J J J J J J

J J J J J J J J J J J J J J J J J J J J J J J J J J

J J J J J J J J J J J J J J J J J J J J J J J J J J

J J J J J J J J J J J J J J J J J J J J J J J J J J

J J J J J J J J J J J J J J J J J J J J J J J J J J

J J J J J J J J J J J J J J J J J J J J J J J J J J

J J J J J J J J J J J J J J J J J J J J J J J J J J

J J J J J J J J J J J J J J J J J J J J J J J J J J

J J J J J J J J J J J J J J J J J J J J J J J J J J

J J J J J J J J J J J J J J J J J J J J J J J J J J

J J J J J J J J J J J J J J J J J J J J J J J J J J

J J J J J J J J J J J J J J J J J J J J J J J J J J

J J J J J J J J J J J J J J J J J J J J J J J J J J

Handwriting font sheet

Nicole Elise Design

K K K K K K K K K K K K K K K K K K K K K K

K K K K K K K K K K K K K K K K K K K K K K

K K K K K K K K K K K K K K K K K K K K K K

K K K K K K K K K K K K K K K K K K K K K K

K K K K K K K K K K K K K K K K K K K K K K

K K K K K K K K K K K K K K K K K K K K K K

K K K K K K K K K K K K K K K K K K K K K K

K K K K K K K K K K K K K K K K K K K K K K

K K K K K K K K K K K K K K K K K K K K K K

K K K K K K K K K K K K K K K K K K K K K K

K K K K K K K K K K K K K K K K K K K K K K

K K K K K K K K K K K K K K K K K K K K K K

K K K K K K K K K K K K K K K K K K K K K K

K K K K K K K K K K K K K K K K K K K K K K

K K K K K K K K K K K K K K K K K K K K K K

K K K K K K K K K K K K K K K K K K K K K K

Handwriting font sheet

Nicole Elise Design

L L L L L L L L L L L L L L L L L L L L L L L L L L L L L
L L L L L L L L L L L L L L L L L L L L L L L L L L L L L
L L L L L L L L L L L L L L L L L L L L L L L L L L L L L
L L L L L L L L L L L L L L L L L L L L L L L L L L L L L
L L L L L L L L L L L L L L L L L L L L L L L L L L L L L
L L L L L L L L L L L L L L L L L L L L L L L L L L L L L
L L L L L L L L L L L L L L L L L L L L L L L L L L L L L
L L L L L L L L L L L L L L L L L L L L L L L L L L L L L
L L L L L L L L L L L L L L L L L L L L L L L L L L L L L
L L L L L L L L L L L L L L L L L L L L L L L L L L L L L
L L L L L L L L L L L L L L L L L L L L L L L L L L L L L
L L L L L L L L L L L L L L L L L L L L L L L L L L L L L
L L L L L L L L L L L L L L L L L L L L L L L L L L L L L
L L L L L L L L L L L L L L L L L L L L L L L L L L L L L
L L L L L L L L L L L L L L L L L L L L L L L L L L L L L
L L L L L L L L L L L L L L L L L L L L L L L L L L L L L
L L L L L L L L L L L L L L L L L L L L L L L L L L L L L

Handwriting font sheet

Nicole Elise Design

m m m m m m m m m m m m m m m m m m m m m

m m m m m m m m m m m m m m m m m m m m m

m m m m m m m m m m m m m m m m m m m m m

m m m m m m m m m m m m m m m m m m m m m

m m m m m m m m m m m m m m m m m m m m m

m m m m m m m m m m m m m m m m m m m m m

m m m m m m m m m m m m m m m m m m m m m

m m m m m m m m m m m m m m m m m m m m m

m m m m m m m m m m m m m m m m m m m m m

m m m m m m m m m m m m m m m m m m m m m

m m m m m m m m m m m m m m m m m m m m m

m m m m m m m m m m m m m m m m m m m m m

m m m m m m m m m m m m m m m m m m m m m

m m m m m m m m m m m m m m m m m m m m m

m m m m m m m m m m m m m m m m m m m m m

m m m m m m m m m m m m m m m m m m m m m

m m m m m m m m m m m m m m m m m m m m m

Handwriting font sheet

Nicole Elise Design

N N N N N N N N N N N N N N N N N N N
N N N N N N N N N N N N N N N N N N N
N N N N N N N N N N N N N N N N N N N
N N N N N N N N N N N N N N N N N N N
N N N N N N N N N N N N N N N N N N N
N N N N N N N N N N N N N N N N N N N
N N N N N N N N N N N N N N N N N N N
N N N N N N N N N N N N N N N N N N N
N N N N N N N N N N N N N N N N N N N
N N N N N N N N N N N N N N N N N N N
N N N N N N N N N N N N N N N N N N N
N N N N N N N N N N N N N N N N N N N
N N N N N N N N N N N N N N N N N N N
N N N N N N N N N N N N N N N N N N N
N N N N N N N N N N N N N N N N N N N
N N N N N N N N N N N N N N N N N N N

Handwriting font sheet

—— Nicole Elise Design ——

0 0 0 0 0 0 0 0 0 0 0 0 0 0 0 0 0 0 0 0 0 0 0

0 0 0 0 0 0 0 0 0 0 0 0 0 0 0 0 0 0 0 0 0 0 0

0 0 0 0 0 0 0 0 0 0 0 0 0 0 0 0 0 0 0 0 0 0 0

0 0 0 0 0 0 0 0 0 0 0 0 0 0 0 0 0 0 0 0 0 0 0

0 0 0 0 0 0 0 0 0 0 0 0 0 0 0 0 0 0 0 0 0 0 0

0 0 0 0 0 0 0 0 0 0 0 0 0 0 0 0 0 0 0 0 0 0 0

0 0 0 0 0 0 0 0 0 0 0 0 0 0 0 0 0 0 0 0 0 0 0

0 0 0 0 0 0 0 0 0 0 0 0 0 0 0 0 0 0 0 0 0 0 0

0 0 0 0 0 0 0 0 0 0 0 0 0 0 0 0 0 0 0 0 0 0 0

0 0 0 0 0 0 0 0 0 0 0 0 0 0 0 0 0 0 0 0 0 0 0

0 0 0 0 0 0 0 0 0 0 0 0 0 0 0 0 0 0 0 0 0 0 0

0 0 0 0 0 0 0 0 0 0 0 0 0 0 0 0 0 0 0 0 0 0 0

0 0 0 0 0 0 0 0 0 0 0 0 0 0 0 0 0 0 0 0 0 0 0

0 0 0 0 0 0 0 0 0 0 0 0 0 0 0 0 0 0 0 0 0 0 0

0 0 0 0 0 0 0 0 0 0 0 0 0 0 0 0 0 0 0 0 0 0 0

0 0 0 0 0 0 0 0 0 0 0 0 0 0 0 0 0 0 0 0 0 0 0

Handwriting font sheet

Nicole Elise Design

P P P P P P P P P P P P P P P P P P P P P P P

P P P P P P P P P P P P P P P P P P P P P P P

P P P P P P P P P P P P P P P P P P P P P P P

P P P P P P P P P P P P P P P P P P P P P P P

P P P P P P P P P P P P P P P P P P P P P P P

P P P P P P P P P P P P P P P P P P P P P P P

P P P P P P P P P P P P P P P P P P P P P P P

P P P P P P P P P P P P P P P P P P P P P P P

P P P P P P P P P P P P P P P P P P P P P P P

P P P P P P P P P P P P P P P P P P P P P P P

P P P P P P P P P P P P P P P P P P P P P P P

P P P P P P P P P P P P P P P P P P P P P P P

P P P P P P P P P P P P P P P P P P P P P P P

P P P P P P P P P P P P P P P P P P P P P P P

P P P P P P P P P P P P P P P P P P P P P P P

P P P P P P P P P P P P P P P P P P P P P P P

Handwriting font sheet

—— Nicole Elise Design ——

Q Q Q Q Q Q Q Q Q Q Q Q Q Q Q Q Q Q Q Q Q Q Q Q Q

Q Q Q Q Q Q Q Q Q Q Q Q Q Q Q Q Q Q Q Q Q Q Q Q Q

Q Q Q Q Q Q Q Q Q Q Q Q Q Q Q Q Q Q Q Q Q Q Q Q Q

Q Q Q Q Q Q Q Q Q Q Q Q Q Q Q Q Q Q Q Q Q Q Q Q Q

Q Q Q Q Q Q Q Q Q Q Q Q Q Q Q Q Q Q Q Q Q Q Q Q Q

Q Q Q Q Q Q Q Q Q Q Q Q Q Q Q Q Q Q Q Q Q Q Q Q Q

Q Q Q Q Q Q Q Q Q Q Q Q Q Q Q Q Q Q Q Q Q Q Q Q Q

Q Q Q Q Q Q Q Q Q Q Q Q Q Q Q Q Q Q Q Q Q Q Q Q Q

Q Q Q Q Q Q Q Q Q Q Q Q Q Q Q Q Q Q Q Q Q Q Q Q Q

Q Q Q Q Q Q Q Q Q Q Q Q Q Q Q Q Q Q Q Q Q Q Q Q Q

Q Q Q Q Q Q Q Q Q Q Q Q Q Q Q Q Q Q Q Q Q Q Q Q Q

Q Q Q Q Q Q Q Q Q Q Q Q Q Q Q Q Q Q Q Q Q Q Q Q Q

Q Q Q Q Q Q Q Q Q Q Q Q Q Q Q Q Q Q Q Q Q Q Q Q Q

Q Q Q Q Q Q Q Q Q Q Q Q Q Q Q Q Q Q Q Q Q Q Q Q Q

Q Q Q Q Q Q Q Q Q Q Q Q Q Q Q Q Q Q Q Q Q Q Q Q Q

Q Q Q Q Q Q Q Q Q Q Q Q Q Q Q Q Q Q Q Q Q Q Q Q Q

Q Q Q Q Q Q Q Q Q Q Q Q Q Q Q Q Q Q Q Q Q Q Q Q Q

Handwriting font sheet

—— Nicole Elise Design ——

R R R R R R R R R R R R R R R R R R R R R
R R R R R R R R R R R R R R R R R R R R R
R R R R R R R R R R R R R R R R R R R R R
R R R R R R R R R R R R R R R R R R R R R
R R R R R R R R R R R R R R R R R R R R R
R R R R R R R R R R R R R R R R R R R R R
R R R R R R R R R R R R R R R R R R R R R
R R R R R R R R R R R R R R R R R R R R R
R R R R R R R R R R R R R R R R R R R R R
R R R R R R R R R R R R R R R R R R R R R
R R R R R R R R R R R R R R R R R R R R R
R R R R R R R R R R R R R R R R R R R R R
R R R R R R R R R R R R R R R R R R R R R
R R R R R R R R R R R R R R R R R R R R R
R R R R R R R R R R R R R R R R R R R R R
R R R R R R R R R R R R R R R R R R R R R
R R R R R R R R R R R R R R R R R R R R R

Handwriting font sheet

S S S S S S S S S S S S S S S S S S S S

S S S S S S S S S S S S S S S S S S S S

S S S S S S S S S S S S S S S S S S S S

S S S S S S S S S S S S S S S S S S S S

S S S S S S S S S S S S S S S S S S S S

S S S S S S S S S S S S S S S S S S S S

S S S S S S S S S S S S S S S S S S S S

S S S S S S S S S S S S S S S S S S S S

S S S S S S S S S S S S S S S S S S S S

S S S S S S S S S S S S S S S S S S S S

S S S S S S S S S S S S S S S S S S S S

S S S S S S S S S S S S S S S S S S S S

S S S S S S S S S S S S S S S S S S S S

S S S S S S S S S S S S S S S S S S S S

S S S S S S S S S S S S S S S S S S S S

S S S S S S S S S S S S S S S S S S S S

S S S S S S S S S S S S S S S S S S S S

Handwriting font sheet

Nicole Elise Design

T T T T T T T T T T T T T T T T T T
T T T T T T T T T T T T T T T T T T
T T T T T T T T T T T T T T T T T T
T T T T T T T T T T T T T T T T T T
T T T T T T T T T T T T T T T T T T
T T T T T T T T T T T T T T T T T T
T T T T T T T T T T T T T T T T T T
T T T T T T T T T T T T T T T T T T
T T T T T T T T T T T T T T T T T T
T T T T T T T T T T T T T T T T T T
T T T T T T T T T T T T T T T T T T
T T T T T T T T T T T T T T T T T T
T T T T T T T T T T T T T T T T T T
T T T T T T T T T T T T T T T T T T
T T T T T T T T T T T T T T T T T T
T T T T T T T T T T T T T T T T T T

Handwriting font sheet

U U U U U U U U U U U U U U U U U U U U U U U U
U U U U U U U U U U U U U U U U U U U U U U U U
U U U U U U U U U U U U U U U U U U U U U U U U
U U U U U U U U U U U U U U U U U U U U U U U U
U U U U U U U U U U U U U U U U U U U U U U U U
U U U U U U U U U U U U U U U U U U U U U U U U
U U U U U U U U U U U U U U U U U U U U U U U U
U U U U U U U U U U U U U U U U U U U U U U U U
U U U U U U U U U U U U U U U U U U U U U U U U
U U U U U U U U U U U U U U U U U U U U U U U U
U U U U U U U U U U U U U U U U U U U U U U U U
U U U U U U U U U U U U U U U U U U U U U U U U
U U U U U U U U U U U U U U U U U U U U U U U U
U U U U U U U U U U U U U U U U U U U U U U U U
U U U U U U U U U U U U U U U U U U U U U U U U
U U U U U U U U U U U U U U U U U U U U U U U U
U U U U U U U U U U U U U U U U U U U U U U U U

—— Nicole Elise Design ——

V V V V V V V V V V V V V V V V V V V V V V V V

V V V V V V V V V V V V V V V V V V V V V V V V

V V V V V V V V V V V V V V V V V V V V V V V V

V V V V V V V V V V V V V V V V V V V V V V V V

V V V V V V V V V V V V V V V V V V V V V V V V

V V V V V V V V V V V V V V V V V V V V V V V V

V V V V V V V V V V V V V V V V V V V V V V V V

V V V V V V V V V V V V V V V V V V V V V V V V

V V V V V V V V V V V V V V V V V V V V V V V V

V V V V V V V V V V V V V V V V V V V V V V V V

V V V V V V V V V V V V V V V V V V V V V V V V

V V V V V V V V V V V V V V V V V V V V V V V V

V V V V V V V V V V V V V V V V V V V V V V V V

V V V V V V V V V V V V V V V V V V V V V V V V

V V V V V V V V V V V V V V V V V V V V V V V V

V V V V V V V V V V V V V V V V V V V V V V V V

Handwriting font sheet

—— Nicole Elise Design ——

W W W W W W W W W W W W W W W W W W W W W W W W W W W W

W W W W W W W W W W W W W W W W W W W W W W W W W W W W

W W W W W W W W W W W W W W W W W W W W W W W W W W W W

W W W W W W W W W W W W W W W W W W W W W W W W W W W W

W W W W W W W W W W W W W W W W W W W W W W W W W W W W

W W W W W W W W W W W W W W W W W W W W W W W W W W W W

W W W W W W W W W W W W W W W W W W W W W W W W W W W W

W W W W W W W W W W W W W W W W W W W W W W W W W W W W

W W W W W W W W W W W W W W W W W W W W W W W W W W W W

W W W W W W W W W W W W W W W W W W W W W W W W W W W W

W W W W W W W W W W W W W W W W W W W W W W W W W W W W

W W W W W W W W W W W W W W W W W W W W W W W W W W W W

W W W W W W W W W W W W W W W W W W W W W W W W W W W W

W W W W W W W W W W W W W W W W W W W W W W W W W W W W

W W W W W W W W W W W W W W W W W W W W W W W W W W W W

W W W W W W W W W W W W W W W W W W W W W W W W W W W W

Handwriting font sheet

Nicole Elise Design

X X X X X X X X X X X X X X X X X X X X X X X X

X X X X X X X X X X X X X X X X X X X X X X X X

X X X X X X X X X X X X X X X X X X X X X X X X

X X X X X X X X X X X X X X X X X X X X X X X X

X X X X X X X X X X X X X X X X X X X X X X X X

X X X X X X X X X X X X X X X X X X X X X X X X

X X X X X X X X X X X X X X X X X X X X X X X X

X X X X X X X X X X X X X X X X X X X X X X X X

X X X X X X X X X X X X X X X X X X X X X X X X

X X X X X X X X X X X X X X X X X X X X X X X X

X X X X X X X X X X X X X X X X X X X X X X X X

X X X X X X X X X X X X X X X X X X X X X X X X

X X X X X X X X X X X X X X X X X X X X X X X X

X X X X X X X X X X X X X X X X X X X X X X X X

X X X X X X X X X X X X X X X X X X X X X X X X

Handwriting font sheet

Nicole Elise Design

Y Y Y Y Y Y Y Y Y Y Y Y Y Y Y Y Y Y Y Y

Y Y Y Y Y Y Y Y Y Y Y Y Y Y Y Y Y Y Y Y

Y Y Y Y Y Y Y Y Y Y Y Y Y Y Y Y Y Y Y Y

Y Y Y Y Y Y Y Y Y Y Y Y Y Y Y Y Y Y Y Y

Y Y Y Y Y Y Y Y Y Y Y Y Y Y Y Y Y Y Y Y

Y Y Y Y Y Y Y Y Y Y Y Y Y Y Y Y Y Y Y Y

Y Y Y Y Y Y Y Y Y Y Y Y Y Y Y Y Y Y Y Y

Y Y Y Y Y Y Y Y Y Y Y Y Y Y Y Y Y Y Y Y

Y Y Y Y Y Y Y Y Y Y Y Y Y Y Y Y Y Y Y Y

Y Y Y Y Y Y Y Y Y Y Y Y Y Y Y Y Y Y Y Y

Y Y Y Y Y Y Y Y Y Y Y Y Y Y Y Y Y Y Y Y

Y Y Y Y Y Y Y Y Y Y Y Y Y Y Y Y Y Y Y Y

Y Y Y Y Y Y Y Y Y Y Y Y Y Y Y Y Y Y Y Y

Y Y Y Y Y Y Y Y Y Y Y Y Y Y Y Y Y Y Y Y

Y Y Y Y Y Y Y Y Y Y Y Y Y Y Y Y Y Y Y Y

Y Y Y Y Y Y Y Y Y Y Y Y Y Y Y Y Y Y Y Y

Y Y Y Y Y Y Y Y Y Y Y Y Y Y Y Y Y Y Y Y

Handwriting font sheet

Nicole Elise Design

Z Z Z Z Z Z Z Z Z Z Z Z Z Z Z Z Z Z Z Z Z Z Z Z Z Z Z

Z Z Z Z Z Z Z Z Z Z Z Z Z Z Z Z Z Z Z Z Z Z Z Z Z Z Z

Z Z Z Z Z Z Z Z Z Z Z Z Z Z Z Z Z Z Z Z Z Z Z Z Z Z Z

Z Z Z Z Z Z Z Z Z Z Z Z Z Z Z Z Z Z Z Z Z Z Z Z Z Z Z

Z Z Z Z Z Z Z Z Z Z Z Z Z Z Z Z Z Z Z Z Z Z Z Z Z Z Z

Z Z Z Z Z Z Z Z Z Z Z Z Z Z Z Z Z Z Z Z Z Z Z Z Z Z Z

Z Z Z Z Z Z Z Z Z Z Z Z Z Z Z Z Z Z Z Z Z Z Z Z Z Z Z

Z Z Z Z Z Z Z Z Z Z Z Z Z Z Z Z Z Z Z Z Z Z Z Z Z Z Z

Z Z Z Z Z Z Z Z Z Z Z Z Z Z Z Z Z Z Z Z Z Z Z Z Z Z Z

Z Z Z Z Z Z Z Z Z Z Z Z Z Z Z Z Z Z Z Z Z Z Z Z Z Z Z

Z Z Z Z Z Z Z Z Z Z Z Z Z Z Z Z Z Z Z Z Z Z Z Z Z Z Z

Z Z Z Z Z Z Z Z Z Z Z Z Z Z Z Z Z Z Z Z Z Z Z Z Z Z Z

Z Z Z Z Z Z Z Z Z Z Z Z Z Z Z Z Z Z Z Z Z Z Z Z Z Z Z

Z Z Z Z Z Z Z Z Z Z Z Z Z Z Z Z Z Z Z Z Z Z Z Z Z Z Z

Z Z Z Z Z Z Z Z Z Z Z Z Z Z Z Z Z Z Z Z Z Z Z Z Z Z Z

Z Z Z Z Z Z Z Z Z Z Z Z Z Z Z Z Z Z Z Z Z Z Z Z Z Z Z

Combined Letter Practice

Handwriting font sheet

Nicole Elise Design

a a a a a a a a a a a a a a a a a a a a a a a a a a a

b b b b b b b b b b b b b b b b b b b b b b b b b b b

c c c c c c c c c c c c c c c c c c c c c c c c c c c

d d d d d d d d d d d d d d d d d d d d d d d d d d d

e e e e e e e e e e e e e e e e e e e e e e e e e e e

f f f f f f f f f f f f f f f f f f f f f f f f f f f

g g g g g g g g g g g g g g g g g g g g g g g g g g g

h h h h h h h h h h h h h h h h h h h h h h h h h h h

i i i i i i i i i i i i i i i i i i i i i i i i i i i

j j j j j j j j j j j j j j j j j j j j j j j j j j j

k k k k k k k k k k k k k k k k k k k k k k k k k k k

l l l l l l l l l l l l l l l l l l l l l l l l l l l

m m m m m m m m m m m m m m m m m m m m m m m m m m m

n n n n n n n n n n n n n n n n n n n n n n n n n n n

o o o o o o o o o o o o o o o o o o o o o o o o o o o

p p p p p p p p p p p p p p p p p p p p p p p p p p p

q q q q q q q q q q q q q q q q q q q q q q q q q q q

Handwriting font sheet

r r r r r r r r r r r r r r r r r r r r r r r r r

s s s s s s s s s s s s s s s s s s s s s s s s s

t t t t t t t t t t t t t t t t t t t t t t t t t

u u u u u u u u u u u u u u u u u u u u u u u u u

v v v v v v v v v v v v v v v v v v v v v v v v v

w w w w w w w w w w w w w w w w w w w w w w w w w

x x x x x x x x x x x x x x x x x x x x x x x x x

y y y y y y y y y y y y y y y y y y y y y y y y y

ʒ ʒ

Handwriting font sheet

Nicole Elise Design

A A A A A A A A A A A A A A A A A A A A A A A A A A A A

B B B B B B B B B B B B B B B B B B B B B B B B B B B B

C C C C C C C C C C C C C C C C C C C C C C C C C C C

D D D D D D D D D D D D D D D D D D D D D D D D D D D D

E E E E E E E E E E E E E E E E E E E E E E E E E E E E

F F F F F F F F F F F F F F F F F F F F F F F F F F F F

G G G G G G G G G G G G G G G G G G G G G G G G G G G

H H H H H H H H H H H H H H H H H H H H H H H H H H H

I I I I I I I I I I I I I I I I I I I I I I I I I I I I

J J J J J J J J J J J J J J J J J J J J J J J J J J J J

K K K K K K K K K K K K K K K K K K K K K K K K K K K

L L L L L L L L L L L L L L L L L L L L L L L L L L L L

M M M M M M M M M M M M M M M M M M M M M M M M M M M

N N N N N N N N N N N N N N N N N N N N N N N N N N N

O O O O O O O O O O O O O O O O O O O O O O O O O O O O

P P P P P P P P P P P P P P P P P P P P P P P P P P P P

Q Q Q Q Q Q Q Q Q Q Q Q Q Q Q Q Q Q Q Q Q Q Q Q Q Q Q Q

Handwriting font sheet

Nicole Elise Design

R R R R R R R R R R R R R R R R R R R R R R R R

S S S S S S S S S S S S S S S S S S S S S S S S

T T T T T T T T T T T T T T T T T T T T T T T T

U U U U U U U U U U U U U U U U U U U U U U U U

V V V V V V V V V V V V V V V V V V V V V V V V

W W W W W W W W W W W W W W W W W W W W W W W W

X X X X X X X X X X X X X X X X X X X X X X X X

Y Y Y Y Y Y Y Y Y Y Y Y Y Y Y Y Y Y Y Y Y Y Y Y

Z Z Z Z Z Z Z Z Z Z Z Z Z Z Z Z Z Z Z Z Z Z Z Z

Handwriting font sheet

Nicole Elise Design

Practice letters.	Your turn!	Practice letters.	Your turn!
a a a a a		n n n n n	
b b b b b		o o o o o	
c c c c c		p p p p p	
d d d d d		q q q q q	
e e e e e		r r r r r	
f f f f f		s s s s s	
g g g g g		t t t t t	
h h h h h		u u u u u	
i i i i i i		v v v v v	
j j j j j		w w w w w	
k k k k k		x x x x x	
l l l l l l		y y y y y	
m m m m m		з з з з з	

Handwriting font sheet

Nicole Elise Design

Practice letters.	Your turn!	Practice letters.	Your turn!
A A A A A		N N N N	
B B B B B		O O O O O	
C C C C C		P P P P P	
D D D D D		Q Q Q Q Q	
E E E E E		R R R R R	
F F F F F		S S S S S	
G G G G G		T T T T T	
H H H H H		U U U U U	
I I I I I I		V V V V V	
J J J J J J		W W W W W	
K K K K K		X X X X X	
L L L L L L		Y Y Y Y Y	
M M M M M		Z Z Z Z Z	

Handwriting font sheet

Nicole Elise Design

abcdefghijklmnopqrstuvwxyz

ABCDEFGHIJKLMNOPQRSTUVWXYZ

abcdefghijklmnopqrstuvwxyz

ABCDEFGHIJKLMNOPQRSTUVWXYZ

abcdefghijklmnopqrstuvwxyz

ABCDEFGHIJKLMNOPQRSTUVWXYZ

abcdefghijklmnopqrstuvwxyz

ABCDEFGHIJKLMNOPQRSTUVWXYZ

abcdefghijklmnopqrstuvwxyz

ABCDEFGHIJKLMNOPQRSTUVWXYZ

abcdefghijklmnopqrstuvwxyz

ABCDEFGHIJKLMNOPQRSTUVWXYZ

abcdefghijklmnopqrstuvwxyz

ABCDEFGHIJKLMNOPQRSTUVWXYZ

Handwriting font sheet

Nicole Elise Design

Aa Aa Aa Aa Aa Aa Aa Aa Aa Aa Aa Aa

Bb Bb Bb Bb Bb Bb Bb Bb Bb Bb Bb Bb

Cc Cc Cc Cc Cc Cc Cc Cc Cc Cc Cc Cc Cc

Dd Dd Dd Dd Dd Dd Dd Dd Dd Dd Dd Dd Dd

Ee Ee Ee Ee Ee Ee Ee Ee Ee Ee Ee Ee Ee

Ff Ff Ff Ff Ff Ff Ff Ff Ff Ff Ff Ff Ff Ff

Gg Gg Gg Gg Gg Gg Gg Gg Gg Gg Gg Gg Gg

Hh Hh Hh Hh Hh Hh Hh Hh Hh Hh Hh Hh Hh

Ii Ii Ii Ii Ii Ii Ii Ii Ii Ii Ii Ii Ii Ii Ii Ii Ii Ii

Jj Jj Jj Jj Jj Jj Jj Jj Jj Jj Jj Jj Jj Jj Jj Jj Jj

Kk Kk Kk Kk Kk Kk Kk Kk Kk Kk Kk Kk Kk

Ll Ll Ll Ll Ll Ll Ll Ll Ll Ll Ll Ll Ll Ll Ll Ll Ll

Mm Mm Mm Mm Mm Mm Mm Mm Mm Mm Mm Mm

Handwriting font sheet

Nicole Elise Design

Nn Nn Nn Nn Nn Nn Nn Nn Nn Nn Nn Nn

Oo Oo Oo Oo Oo Oo Oo Oo Oo Oo Oo Oo Oo

Pp Pp Pp Pp Pp Pp Pp Pp Pp Pp Pp Pp Pp

Qq Qq Qq Qq Qq Qq Qq Qq Qq Qq Qq Qq

Rr Rr Rr Rr Rr Rr Rr Rr Rr Rr Rr Rr Rr Rr

Ss Ss Ss Ss Ss Ss Ss Ss Ss Ss Ss Ss Ss Ss

Tt Tt Tt Tt Tt Tt Tt Tt Tt Tt Tt Tt Tt Tt

Uu Uu Uu Uu Uu Uu Uu Uu Uu Uu Uu Uu Uu

Vv Vv Vv Vv Vv Vv Vv Vv Vv Vv Vv Vv Vv Vv

Ww Ww Ww Ww Ww Ww Ww Ww Ww Ww Ww

Xx Xx Xx Xx Xx Xx Xx Xx Xx Xx Xx Xx Xx Xx

Yy Yy Yy Yy Yy Yy Yy Yy Yy Yy Yy Yy Yy Yy

Zz Zz Zz Zz Zz Zz Zz Zz Zz Zz Zz Zz Zz Zz

Handwriting font sheet

By Nicole Elise

Aa Aa Aa Aa Aa Aa Aa Aa Aa Aa Aa Aa Aa Aa

Bb Bb Bb Bb Bb Bb Bb Bb Bb Bb Bb Bb Bb Bb

Cc Cc Cc Cc Cc Cc Cc Cc Cc Cc Cc Cc Cc Cc Cc

Dd Dd Dd Dd Dd Dd Dd Dd Dd Dd Dd Dd Dd Dd

Ee Ee Ee Ee Ee Ee Ee Ee Ee Ee Ee Ee Ee Ee Ee

Ff Ff Ff Ff Ff Ff Ff Ff Ff Ff Ff Ff Ff Ff Ff

Gg Gg Gg Gg Gg Gg Gg Gg Gg Gg Gg Gg Gg Gg Gg

Hh Hh Hh Hh Hh Hh Hh Hh Hh Hh Hh Hh

Handwriting font sheet

By Nicole Elise

Ii Ii Ii Ii Ii Ii Ii Ii Ii Ii Ii Ii Ii Ii Ii Ii Ii Ii

Jj Jj Jj Jj Jj Jj Jj Jj Jj Jj Jj Jj Jj Jj Jj Jj Jj Jj

Kk Kk Kk Kk Kk Kk Kk Kk Kk Kk Kk Kk Kk Kk Kk Kk Kk

Ll Ll Ll Ll Ll Ll Ll Ll Ll Ll Ll Ll Ll Ll Ll Ll Ll Ll

Mm Mm Mm Mm Mm Mm Mm Mm Mm Mm Mm Mm Mm Mm

Nn Nn Nn Nn Nn Nn Nn Nn Nn Nn Nn Nn Nn Nn

Oo Oo Oo Oo Oo Oo Oo Oo Oo Oo Oo Oo Oo Oo Oo Oo

Pp Pp Pp Pp Pp Pp Pp Pp Pp Pp Pp Pp Pp Pp Pp Pp

Handwriting font sheet

By Nicole Elise

Qq Qq Qq Qq Qq Qq Qq Qq Qq Qq Qq Qq Qq Qq

Rr Rr Rr Rr Rr Rr Rr Rr Rr Rr Rr Rr Rr Rr Rr

Ss Ss Ss Ss Ss Ss Ss Ss Ss Ss Ss Ss Ss Ss Ss

Tt Tt Tt Tt Tt Tt Tt Tt Tt Tt Tt Tt Tt Tt Tt

Uu Uu Uu Uu Uu Uu Uu Uu Uu Uu Uu Uu Uu Uu Uu

Vv Vv Vv Vv Vv Vv Vv Vv Vv Vv Vv Vv Vv Vv Vv

Ww Ww Ww Ww Ww Ww Ww Ww Ww Ww Ww Ww Ww Ww

Handwriting font sheet

By Nicole Elise

Xx Xx Xx Xx Xx Xx Xx Xx Xx Xx Xx Xx Xx Xx

Yy Yy Yy Yy Yy Yy Yy Yy Yy Yy Yy Yy Yy Yy

Zz Zz Zz Zz Zz Zz Zz Zz Zz Zz Zz Zz Zz Zz

Your turn!

Numbers Practice

Handwriting font sheet

Nicole Elise Design

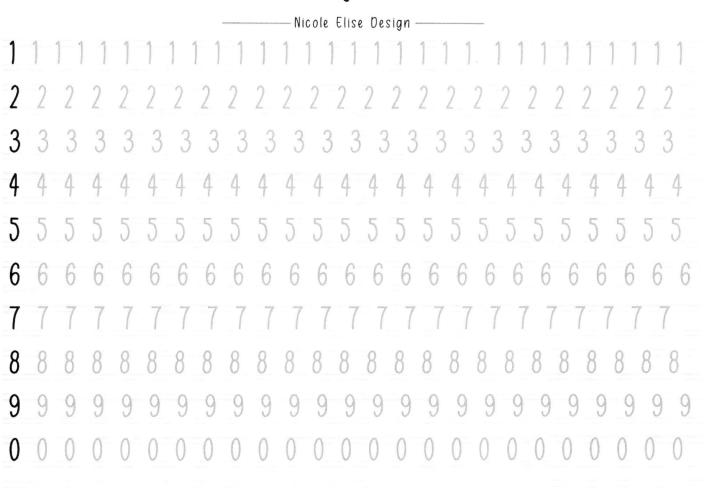

1 1 1 1 1 1 1 1 1 1 1 1 1 1 1 1 1 1 1 1 1 1 1 1 1 1 1 1 1 1 1 1

2 2 2 2 2 2 2 2 2 2 2 2 2 2 2 2 2 2 2 2 2 2 2 2 2 2 2 2 2 2 2

3 3 3 3 3 3 3 3 3 3 3 3 3 3 3 3 3 3 3 3 3 3 3 3 3 3 3 3 3 3 3

4 4 4 4 4 4 4 4 4 4 4 4 4 4 4 4 4 4 4 4 4 4 4 4 4 4 4 4 4 4 4

5 5 5 5 5 5 5 5 5 5 5 5 5 5 5 5 5 5 5 5 5 5 5 5 5 5 5 5 5 5 5

6 6 6 6 6 6 6 6 6 6 6 6 6 6 6 6 6 6 6 6 6 6 6 6 6 6 6 6 6 6 6

7 7 7 7 7 7 7 7 7 7 7 7 7 7 7 7 7 7 7 7 7 7 7 7 7 7 7 7 7 7 7

8 8 8 8 8 8 8 8 8 8 8 8 8 8 8 8 8 8 8 8 8 8 8 8 8 8 8 8 8 8 8

9 9 9 9 9 9 9 9 9 9 9 9 9 9 9 9 9 9 9 9 9 9 9 9 9 9 9 9 9 9 9

0 0 0 0 0 0 0 0 0 0 0 0 0 0 0 0 0 0 0 0 0 0 0 0 0 0 0 0 0 0 0

Handwriting font sheet

By Nicole Elise

1 2 3 4 5 6 7 8 9 0

1 2 3 4 5 6 7 8 9 0

1 2 3 4 5 6 7 8 9 0

1 2 3 4 5 6 7 8 9 0

1 2 3 4 5 6 7 8 9 0

1 2 3 4 5 6 7 8 9 0

1 2 3 4 5 6 7 8 9 0

1 2 3 4 5 6 7 8 9 0

1 2 3 4 5 6 7 8 9 0

1 2 3 4 5 6 7 8 9 0

98345009876543234782017346123491347070982513509 2352

21346142712401401242342340257245903450345734517234714

12479023509823465835241937465930173454238101029 38465

81033141458609287651920432058451238134813461247 1340845

23429023018134042713461470981401873498708734891 3190123

Extra Word Practice

Handwriting font sheet

Nicole Elise Design

the quick brown fox jumps over the lazy dog

the quick brown fox jumps over the lazy dog

the quick brown fox jumps over the lazy dog

the quick brown fox jumps over the lazy dog

the quick brown fox jumps over the lazy dog

the quick brown fox jumps over the lazy dog

the quick brown fox jumps over the lazy dog

the quick brown fox jumps over the lazy dog

the quick brown fox jumps over the lazy dog

the quick brown fox jumps over the lazy dog

the quick brown fox jumps over the lazy dog

the quick brown fox jumps over the lazy dog

the quick brown fox jumps over the lazy dog

the quick brown fox jumps over the lazy dog

the quick brown fox jumps over the lazy dog

the quick brown fox jumps over the lazy dog

Handwriting font sheet

Nicole Elise Design

THE QUICK BROWN FOX JUMPS OVER THE LAZY DOG

THE QUICK BROWN FOX JUMPS OVER THE LAZY DOG

THE QUICK BROWN FOX JUMPS OVER THE LAZY DOG

THE QUICK BROWN FOX JUMPS OVER THE LAZY DOG

THE QUICK BROWN FOX JUMPS OVER THE LAZY DOG

THE QUICK BROWN FOX JUMPS OVER THE LAZY DOG

THE QUICK BROWN FOX JUMPS OVER THE LAZY DOG

THE QUICK BROWN FOX JUMPS OVER THE LAZY DOG

Handwriting font sheet

By Nicole Elise

the quick brown fox jumps over the lazy dog

THE QUICK BROWN FOX JUMPS OVER THE LAZY DOG

the quick brown fox jumps over the lazy dog

THE QUICK BROWN FOX JUMPS OVER THE LAZY DOG

the quick brown fox jumps over the lazy dog

THE QUICK BROWN FOX JUMPS OVER THE LAZY DOG

the quick brown fox jumps over the lazy dog

THE QUICK BROWN FOX JUMPS OVER THE LAZY DOG

the quick brown fox jumps over the lazy dog

THE QUICK BROWN FOX JUMPS OVER THE LAZY DOG

the quick brown fox jumps over the lazy dog

THE QUICK BROWN FOX JUMPS OVER THE LAZY DOG

the quick brown fox jumps over the lazy dog

THE QUICK BROWN FOX JUMPS OVER THE LAZY DOG

Handwriting font sheet

Nicole Elise Design

January January January January January

February February February February

March March March March March March

April April April April April April April April

May May May May May May May May

June June June June June June June June

July July July July July July July July July

August August August August August

September September September September September

October October October October October

November November November November

December December December December

Handwriting font sheet

By Nicole Elise

JANUARY JANUARY JANUARY JANUARY JANUARY

FEBRUARY FEBRUARY FEBRUARY FEBRUARY

MARCH MARCH MARCH MARCH MARCH MARCH

APRIL APRIL APRIL APRIL APRIL APRIL APRIL

MAY MAY MAY MAY MAY MAY MAY MAY

JUNE JUNE JUNE JUNE JUNE JUNE JUNE JUNE

JULY JULY JULY JULY JULY JULY JULY JULY JULY

AUGUST AUGUST AUGUST AUGUST AUGUST

SEPTEMBER SEPTEMBER SEPTEMBER SEPTEMBER

OCTOBER OCTOBER OCTOBER OCTOBER OCTOBER

NOVEMBER NOVEMBER NOVEMBER NOVEMBER

DECEMBER DECEMBER DECEMBER DECEMBER

Handwriting font sheet

By Nicole Elise

monday monday monday monday monday

tuesday tuesday tuesday tuesday tuesday

wednesday   wednesday   wednesday

thursday thursday thursday thursday

friday friday friday friday friday friday

saturday saturday saturday saturday

sunday sunday sunday sunday sunday

Handwriting font sheet

By Nicole Elise

MONDAY MONDAY MONDAY MONDAY MONDAY

TUESDAY TUESDAY TUESDAY TUESDAY TUESDAY

WEDNESDAY WEDNESDAY WEDNESDAY

THURSDAY THURSDAY THURSDAY THURSDAY

FRIDAY FRIDAY FRIDAY FRIDAY FRIDAY FRIDAY

SATURDAY SATURDAY SATURDAY SATURDAY

SUNDAY SUNDAY SUNDAY SUNDAY SUNDAY

Handwriting font sheet

——— Nicole Elise Design ———

The greatest glory in living lies not in never falling, but in rising every time we fall. -Nelson Mandela

The way to get started is to quit talking and begin doing. -Walt Disney

Your time is limited, so don't waste it living someone else's life. Don't be trapped by dogma - which is living with the results of other people's thinking - Steve Jobs. If life were predictable it would cease to be life, and be without flavour - Eleanor Roosevelt

If you look at what you have in life, you'll always have more. If you look at what you don't have in life, you'll never have enough - Oprah Winfrey

Handwriting font sheet

———— Nicole Elise Design ————

If you set your goals ridiculously high and it's a failure, you will fail above everyone else's success. -James Cameron.

Life is what happens when you're busy making other plans. -John Lennon

Spread love everywhere you go. Let no one ever come to you without leaving happier. -Mother Teresa

When you reach the end of your rope, tie a knot in it and hang on. -Franklin D. Roosevelt

Always remember that you are absolutely unique. Just like everyone else. -Margaret Mead

Don't judge each day by the harvest you reap but by the seeds that you plant. -Robert Louis Stevenson

The future belongs to those who believe in the beauty of their dreams. -Eleanor Roosevelt

Handwriting font sheet

—— Nicole Elise Design ——

Tell me and I forget. Teach me and I remember.
Involve me and I learn. -Benjamin Franklin
The best and most beautiful things in the world
cannot be seen or even touched - they must be
felt with the heart. -Helen Keller
It is during our darkest moments that we must
focus to see the light. -Aristotle
Whoever is happy will make others happy too.
-Anne Frank
Do not go where the path may lead. go instead
where there is no path and leave a trail. -Ralph
Waldo Emerson
You will face many defeats in life. but never let
yourself be defeated. -Maya Angelou
The greatest glory in living lies not in never
falling. but in rising every time we fall. -Nelson
Mandela

Handwriting font sheet

—— Nicole Elise Design ——

In the end, it's not the years in your life that count. It's the life in your years. -Abraham Lincoln

Never let the fear of striking out keep you from playing the game. -Babe Ruth

Life is either a daring adventure or nothing at all. -Helen Keller

Many of life's failures are people who did not realize how close they were to success when they gave up. -Thomas A. Edison

You have brains in your head. You have feet in your shoes. You can steer yourself any direction you choose. -Dr. Seuss

Keep smiling, because life is a beautiful thing and there's so much to smile about. -Marilyn Monroe

Handwriting font sheet

Nicole Elise Design

Life is a long lesson in humility. -James M. Barrie

In three words I can sum up everything I've learned about life: it goes on. -Robert Frost

Love the life you live. Live the life you love. -Bob Marley

Life is either a daring adventure or nothing at all. -Helen Keller

You have brains in your head. You have feet in your shoes. You can steer yourself any direction you choose. -Dr. Seuss

Life is made of ever so many partings welded together. -Charles Dickens

Life is trying things to see if they work. -Ray Bradbury

The purpose of our lives is to be happy. - Dalai Lama

Handwriting font sheet

—— Nicole Elise Design ——

Your time is limited. so don't waste it living someone else's life. Don't be trapped by dogma - which is living with the results of other people's thinking. -Steve Jobs

Many of life's failures are people who did not realize how close they were to success when they gave up. -Thomas A. Edison

Don't be distracted by criticism. Remember - the only taste of success some people get is to take a bite out of you. -Zig Ziglar

Life is what happens when you're busy making other plans - John Lennon

Get busy living or get busy dying - Stephen King

You only live once. but if you do it right. once is enough - Mae West

Life is not a problem to be solved. but a reality to be experienced - Soren Kierkegaard

Handwriting font sheet

Nicole Elise Design

Many of life's failures are people who did not realize how close they were to success when they gave up— Thomas A. Edison

Sing like no one's listening. love like you've never been hurt. dance like nobody's watching. and live like it's heaven on earth - (Attributed to various sources)

Curiosity about life in all of its aspects. I think. is still the secret of great creative people - Leo Burnett

The unexamined life is not worth living - Socrates

Turn your wounds into wisdom - Oprah Winfrey

The way I see it. if you want the rainbow. you gotta put up with the rain - Dolly Parton

Handwriting font sheet

———— Nicole Elise Design ————

Don't settle for what life gives you: make life better and build something - Ashton Kutcher

Everybody wants to be famous. but nobody wants to do the work. I live by that. You grind hard so you can play hard. At the end of the day. you put all the work in. and eventually it'll pay off. It could be in a year. it could be in 30 years. Eventually. your hard work will pay off - Kevin Hart

Classical music is one of the best things that ever happened to mankind. If you get introduced to it in the right way. it becomes your friend for life. - Yo Yo Ma

Do all the good you can. for all the people you can. in all the ways you can. as long as you can - Hillary Clinton

Handwriting font sheet

Nicole Elise Design

The first law for the historian is that he shall never dare utter an untruth. The second is that he shall suppress nothing that is true. Moreover, there shall be no suspicion of partiality in his writing, or of malice. - Marcus Tullius Cicero

Life isn't always beautiful. That was a lesson that Dan was learning. He also realized that life wasn't easy. This had come as a shock since he had lived a charmed life. He hated that this was the truth and he struggled to be happy knowing that his assumptions weren't correct. He wouldn't realize until much later in life that the difficult obstacles he was facing that were taking away the beauty in his life at this moment would ultimately make his life much more beautiful. All he knew was that at this moment was that life isn't always beautiful.

Handwriting font sheet

————— Nicole Elise Design —————

The fact that you could never do anything in public without being mobbed and the complete lack of privacy was something that she never wanted to experience. She also had no desire to have strangers speculating about every aspect of her life and what each thing she did was supposed to mean. Brenda was perfectly happy with her anonymous life where she could do exactly as she wanted without anyone else giving a damn. Thus, her overnight Internet celebrity was not something she was thrilled about as her friends told her how lucky she was.

Hopes and dreams were dashed that day. It should have been expected, but it still came as a shock. The warning signs had been ignored in favor of the possibility, however remote, that it could actually happen.

Handwriting font sheet

Nicole Elise Design

Was it enough? That was the question he kept asking himself. Was being satisfied enough? He looked around him at everyone yearning to just be satisfied in their daily life and he had reached that goal. He knew that he was satisfied and he also knew it wasn't going to be enough. Brenda never wanted to be famous. While most of her friends dreamed about being famous. she could see the negative aspects that those who wanted to be famous seemed to ignore.

Handwriting font sheet

By Nicole Elise

Brenda never wanted to be famous. While most of her friends dreamed about being famous. she could see the negative aspects that those who wanted to be famous seemed to ignore. The fact that you could never do anything in public without being mobbed and the complete lack of privacy was something that she never wanted to experience. She also had no desire to have strangers speculating about every aspect of her life and what each thing she did was supposed to mean. Brenda was perfectly happy with her anonymous life where she could do exactly as she wanted without anyone else giving a damn. Thus. her overnight Internet celebrity was not something she was thrilled about as her friends told her how lucky she was

Handwriting font sheet

By Nicole Elise

Hopes and dreams were dashed that day. It should have been expected. but it still came as a shock. The warning signs had been ignored in favor of the possibility. however remote. that it could actually happen. That possibility had grown from hope to an undeniable belief it must be destiny. That was until it wasn't and the hopes and dreams came crashing down.

It was easy to spot her. All you needed to do was look at her socks. They were never a matching pair. One would be green while the other would be blue. One would reach her knee while the other barely touched her ankle. Every other part of her was perfect. but never the socks. They were her micro act of rebellion.

His parents continued to question him. He didn't know what to say to them since they refused to believe the truth. He explained again and again, and they dismissed his explanation as a figment of his imagination. There was no way that grandpa, who had been dead for five years, could have told him where the treasure had been hidden. Of course, it didn't help that grandpa was roaring with laughter in the chair next to him as he tried to explain once again how he'd found it.

Green vines attached to the trunk of the tree had wound themselves toward the top of the canopy. Ants used the vine as their private highway, avoiding all the creases and crags of the bark, to freely move at top speed from top to bottom or bottom to top depending on their current chore. At least this was the way it was supposed to be. Something had damaged the vine overnight halfway up the tree leaving a gap in the once pristine ant highway.

I've rented a car in Las Vegas and have reserved a hotel in Twentynine Palms which is just north of Joshua Tree. We'll drive from Las Vegas through Mojave National Preserve and possibly do a short hike on our way down. Then spend all day on Monday at Joshua Tree. We can decide the next morning if we want to do more in Joshua Tree or Mojave before we head back.

Handwriting font sheet

By Nicole Elise

There was a time and a place for Stephanie to use her magic. The problem was that she had a difficult time determining this. She wished she could simply use it when the desire hit and there wouldn't be any unforeseen consequences. Unfortunately, that's not how it worked and the consequences could be devastating if she accidentally used her magic at the wrong time.

Life is short, always choose kindness
Summer Autumn Fall Winter Spring
Happy birthday to you!
Be determined to dream, live in abundance and need let your fears get in the way of conquering your dreams

Handwriting font sheet

By Nicole Elise

Nearly ten years had passed since the Dursleys had woken up to find their nephew on the front step. but Privet Drive had hardly changed at all. The sun rose on the same tidy front gardens and lit up the brass number four on the Dursleys' front door: it crept into their living room. which was almost exactly the same as it had been on the night when Mr. Dursley had seen that fateful news report about the owls. Only the photographs on the mantelpiece really showed how much time had passed. Ten years ago. there had been lots of pictures of what looked like a large pink beach ball wearing different-colored bonnets - but Dudley Dursley was no longer a baby. and now the photographs showed a large blond boy riding his first bicycle. on a carousel at the fair.

Handwriting font sheet

By Nicole Elise

Grateful thankful confident blessed. I want the world for you. The best and most beautiful things in the world can not be seen or even touched. They must be felt with the heart

Wandering down the path to the pond had become a daily routine. Even when the weather wasn't cooperating like today with the wind and rain. Jerry still took the morning stroll down the path until he reached the pond. Although there didn't seem to be a particular reason Jerry did this to anyone looking in from the outside. those who knew him well knew exactly what was going on. It could all be traced back to a specific incident that happened exactly 5 years previously.

HANDWRITING TIPS

Embrace Your Personal Style

Handwriting is a reflection of your own personal style - maybe every letter isn't exactly like the workbook and that's okay. Consider this handwriting practice just adding to your style. Instead, focus on making clearly formed letters that are easy to read.

PENS

This is a question I get asked a lot. From a gel pen to a regular ballpoint pen, a fountain pen or thicker barrel/ millimetre pen, everyone's preference is different! You have to hunt for the pen that's right for you. I encourage you to shop around. Have a browse over some YouTube videos to see what may suit your needs.

Paper

For paperback versions: You can use a light grey led pencil and erase to start over, or simply buy some tracing paper to utilise the pages over and over again.

For PDF versions: If you're printing double-sided and using a pen that may bleed through, choosing a thicker weight paper (higher LB/GSM weight) can help reduce the amount of visible bleed. I personally find that silk-feel paper is also quite nice to write on.

Posture Makes Perfect

Sit with your feet flat on the floor, straight back and relax your arm and hand. Tilting your paper to write is a personal preference, so do what best suits your personal style here.

Remember To Relax your Grip

You may find that your fingers get really sore when writing for short periods of time when you start. Your fingers shouldn't be white from squeezing the pen too hard.

Slow & Steady Wins The Race

Ever notice how your handwriting looks a little better when you're not writing at 100 miles an hour? Starting slow will help your hands really grasp that muscle memory that you need to consistently write those letters perfectly and make for an overall neater handwriting experience. Don't worry, as soon as that muscle memory kicks in, you will find yourself being able to write a little quicker.

Examine Your Own Writing

When you get confident enough to write on the blank lined sheet page provided (or even free-hand on your own paper! Go you!), take some time to examine your writing and the individual letters. Have a look at the forwards/backward slant, the spacing between the letters, their height, (ascending and descending) and how the letters look compared to how they looked when you were tracing them. Write a couple paragraphs. Circle the letters you're not happy with and compare them to the workbook letters and see what you can improve on.

Practice Practice Practice

Sneak in a practice when you get the chance. Whether it's writing a sticky note or the shopping list - every little bit of practice counts. The more you practice, the better that muscle memory will get.

35 HANDWRITING PROMPTS

1. Write out your favourite song lyrics.
2. Write a letter to your 10-year-old self about what you would give yourself advice on.
3. *WHAT IS SOMETHING YOU ALWAYS THINK 'WHAT IF' ABOUT AND WHY?*
4. *What three lessons do you want your children to learn from you?*
5. Discuss your first love.
6. Write about the first time you met your best friend.
7. *Write about an area of your life that you would like to improve.*
8. What are your goals for the next 30 days?
9. Your highs and lows for the month.
10. What is something quirky that you do that you think no one else can do?
11. *What is a challenge that you would love to tackle?*
12. What are 3 things that you love about your life right now?
13. *Positive affirmations about your body*
14. What is the funniest thing a pet/animal has done? What makes them so funny?
15. Currently, what is causing you stress?
16. **What do you look for in a relationship?**
17. *What sets your heart on fire?*
18. **What do you hate doing? How does it make you feel?**
19. What are your New Years Resolutions?
20. **What is going really well in your life right now?**
21. **What are you most thankful for in life right now?**
22. *IF YOU COULD CHANGE ANYTHING ABOUT YOURSELF, WHAT WOULD IT BE AND WHY?*
23. *What are your favourite things about Christmas time?*
24. *What are your favourite things about fall time?*
25. Describe your perfect day.
26. Write about a song and a feeling it evoked in you.
27. Write about an item you have that isn't expensive but means a lot to you.
28. *What colour do you feel like today and why?*
29. Make a list of your favourite puns
30. *WRITE A MOVIE REVIEW ABOUT THE FUNNIEST MOVIE THAT YOU HAVE EVER SEEN*
31. Imagine that your pet ran your household. Write a short story about what life would be like if your animal was who you had to answer to.
32. Who do you believe is the funniest person in your life. why?
33. *What is something that people from older generations do that you find quirky?*
34. *WRITE A SHORT FUNNY STORY WHERE THE MAIN PERSON IS YOUR ALTER-EGO.*
35. Write a short funny post-apocalyptic story.

Blank Practice Sheet

Handwriting font sheet

By Nicole Elise

Handwriting font sheet

By Nicole Elise

Handwriting font sheet

By Nicole Elise

Made in United States
North Haven, CT
21 September 2023

41806105R00061